Praise for James Oliver and Lois E. Horton's
Slavery and the Making of America

"The Hortons demonstrate their wide mastery of the literature, telling the tragic and triumphant story of the 'peculiar institution' through the words and experiences of the people who lived it."
—Henry Louis Gates, Jr., Harvard University

"The oft-told tale is made fresh through up-to-date slavery scholarship, the extensive use of slave narratives and archival photos and, especially, a focus on individual experience. The well-known players (Attucks, Vesey, Tubman, Douglass) appear, but so do the more anonymous ones—the planter's wife and the slave driver share space with the abolitionist and the Confederate soldier, and all are skillfully etched. As the Hortons chronicle lives from freedom in Africa to slavery in America and beyond, they tell an integral American story, a tale not of juxtaposition but of edgy oneness."
—*Publishers Weekly*

"Shows how the history of American slavery and the history of the American nation are intertwined. Rare illustrations and scrupulous attention to the viewpoint of the slaves make this account especially interesting."
—*The Tampa Tribune*

"Ambitious. . . . Revises the historical record and overturns long-held beliefs about the institution of slavery and what it has meant to the country."
—*The Denver Post* (on PBS companion documentary *Slavery and the Making of America*)

"Dissects the incredible influences of the terrible moral fault in our history."
—*The Nashville City Paper*

"A terrific historical account of the roles and influence that the black slaves made on the United States. The Hortons provide an insightful look on how the slaves impacted all aspects of culture. . . . Anecdotal reciting and photographs augment this superb account. . . . Easy to read but difficult to put down because the book is so engrossing, this is a fabulous tome that history buffs will take immense delight in."
—*The Midwest Book Review*

"An excellent guide to an often difficult subject. Complete with dozens of images, a chronology of events, a list of recommended readings and website suggestions, *Slavery and the Making of America* is an up-to-date book, which offers not only a strong central storyline but also resources for further study."
—*North & South*

"Brings the appalling history of slavery into an especially clear focus by laying out of a fuller, more detailed historical/cultural timeline."
—*The Stamford Advocate*

SLAVERY

AND THE

MAKING of AMERICA

James Oliver Horton

Lois E. Horton

OXFORD
UNIVERSITY PRESS

OXFORD
UNIVERSITY PRESS

Oxford University Press, Inc., publishes works that
further Oxford University's objective of excellence
in research, scholarship, and education.

Oxford   New York
Auckland   Cape Town   Dar es Salaam   Hong Kong   Karachi
Kuala Lumpur   Madrid   Melbourne   Mexico City   Nairobi
New Delhi   Shanghai   Taipei   Toronto

With offices in
Argentina   Austria   Brazil   Chile   Czech Republic   France   Greece
Guatemala   Hungary   Italy   Japan   Poland   Portugal   Singapore
South Korea   Switzerland   Thailand   Turkey   Ukraine   Vietnam

First published by Oxford University Press, Inc., 2005
198 Madison Avenue, New York, NY 10016
www.oup.com

First issued as an Oxford University Press paperback, 2006
ISBN-13: 978-0-19-530451-0
ISBN-10: 0-19-530451-9

Oxford is a registered trademark of Oxford University Press

The Library of Congress has cataloged the cloth edition as follows:

Horton, James Oliver.
Slavery and the making of America / James Oliver Horton and Lois Horton.
p. cm. Includes bibliographical references (p.   ) and index.
ISBN-13: 978-0-19-517903-3   ISBN-10: 0-19-517903-X (acid-free paper)
1. Slavery—United States—History. 2. African Americans—History—To 1863.
I. Horton, Lois E. II. Title.

E441.H73 2004   973'.0496073—dc22   2004013617

Designed and Typeset by Alexis Siroc

1 3 5 7 9 8 6 4 2
Printed in the United States of America
on acid-free paper

Contents

Introduction

Slavery played a profoundly important role in the making of the United States, as the institution grew from the handful of Africans landed in Virginia in 1619 to the four million African Americans held in bondage at the beginning of the Civil War in 1861. The bound labor of at least twelve generations of black people created great wealth for slaveholders, wealth that was translated into extraordinary political power. The slave trade and the products created by slaves' labor, particularly cotton, provided the basis for America's wealth as a nation, underwriting the country's industrial revolution and enabling it to project its power into the rest of the world. African slaves were not simply passive laborers. They brought many new cultures to America, and their religion, music, language, values, and skills helped shape America and its unique blended culture. Enduring a brutally oppressive system, African slaves also developed a deep commitment to liberty and became a living testament to the powerful appeal of freedom.

American slavery profoundly affected the concept and the actual development of American freedom. It provided a touchstone for patriots' demands for liberty and representative government. They believed, as John Dickinson of Pennsylvania claimed in the wake of the Stamp Act Crisis of the 1760s, that "Those who are taxed without their own consent, expressed by themselves or their representatives, are slaves." Because England had taxed the American colonies without their consent, Dickinson continued, "We are therefore–SLAVES." The argument that Britain sought to make Americans slaves in the mid-eighteenth century was a gross exaggeration, but Americans used the term metaphorically to impress Britain with the seriousness of their opposition to the loss of liberty. Dickinson's words carried a great irony when he wrote them in 1768, because he was the largest slaveholder in Philadelphia at the time, and his slaves were bound by chains much stronger than metaphors.[1]

This book is the story of American slavery and of the people whose loss of liberty under its yoke was much more than a deprivation of political representation. It is the story of African people becoming African Americans, for most under unimaginably oppressive and inhumane conditions, often told in their own words. It examines the great contradiction at the heart of American democracy—that a freedom-loving people tolerated human bondage that violated the values they professed to hold dearest. Generation after generation of Americans tried unsuccessfully to reconcile this contradiction, and America's history was shaped by this futile effort. This book is also about the determination of black Americans and their white allies to have the nation live up to the principles embodied in the Declaration of Independence, the Bill of Rights, and the other founding documents of American freedom.

By the time of the Revolution, Americans had wrestled with the meaning of slavery for more than 150 years. Slavery had created a hellish existence for the half million Africans caught in its grip and posed an ethical dilemma for liberal philosophers attempting to explain a slaveholders' revolution for freedom. It also created a struggle between the forces of slavery and the forces of freedom, which finally erupted in a bloody Civil War. Although slavery was at the heart of this conflict, most Americans have yet to understand its importance, the institution of slavery itself, or the lives of the slaves.

In the early twentieth century, popular interpretations of slavery were dominated by novelists, playwrights, and filmmakers whose works were largely based on the Old South view of slavery as a benevolent institution. In 1906 the Reverend Thomas Dixon, a North Carolinian who was pastor of the Twenty-third Street Baptist Church in New York City, published his best-selling novel, *The Clansman,* glorifying the political terrorism of the Ku Klux Klan during the volatile decades of the post–Civil-War Reconstruction era. Dixon's book depicted the Klan as a force for order and the restoration of southern honor. Film director D. W. Griffith brought Dixon's novel to the screen in 1915 in an innovative and powerful movie, *Birth of a Nation.* Screened at the White House and praised by President Woodrow Wilson as "history written with lightening," the film became a sensation, affirming racist assumptions underlying the system of racial segregation that was at its height in the early decades of the twentieth century.[2]

Interpretations of slavery by professional historians have changed over time as new historical sources became available and the times prompted new historical questions. One of the most influential academic historians of the early twentieth century was U. B. Phillips, who was born in Georgia, educated at Columbia University in New York City, and became professor of history and political science at the University of Wisconsin, Tulane University, the University of Michigan, and

Yale University. His portrayal of blacks as passive, inferior people, whose African origins made them uncivilized, seemed to provide historical evidence for the theories of racial inferiority that supported racial segregation. Drawing evidence exclusively from plantation records, letters, southern newspapers, and other sources reflecting the slaveholder's point of view, Phillips depicted slave masters who provided for the welfare of their slaves and contended that true affection existed between slave and master. This interpretation of slavery influenced most textbooks and popular media of the time and was reflected in the 1939 film classic *Gone with the Wind*, derived from Margaret Mitchell's best-selling 1936 historical novel set in the Civil War and Reconstruction periods.[3]

Some historical scholarship attempted to counter popular racist views and the defense of slavery during the 1930s and 1940s, but the benign view of slavery fit with the notion of white supremacy that was solidly entrenched in the society. Finally in 1956, in the wake of post–World War II civil rights protests and changing racial attitudes, historian Kenneth Stampp published a full-blown refutation of the idea of slavery as a benevolent institution. Stampp's book, *The Peculiar Institution: Slavery in the Ante-Bellum South*, was based on many of the same sources that Phillips had used, but it relied more heavily on diaries, journals, newspaper runaway-slave ads, and even a few slave narratives. Comparing slavery to the experience of the victims of World War II concentration camps, Stanley Elkins, in *Slavery*, posited slavery's damaging psychological impact on the personalities of the slaves. He painted a picture of the Sambo personality, child-like, dependent, and silly, as caricatured in minstrel shows. This personality distortion, he said, was created by the almost total helplessness of slaves and their reliance on the slave master.

By the late 1960s the impact of the modern civil rights movement had alerted scholars and many other Americans to the significance of African American history and its tradition of struggle. This raised new questions about the nature and impact of slavery and the response of black people to it. During the 1970s, scholars made greater use of the WPA slave interviews that historians sponsored by the federal government had conducted in the 1930s with the last living generation of former slaves,[4] and of hundreds of slave autobiographies published in the nineteenth century. Such scholars as John Blassingame, in the *Slave Community*, Eugene Genovese, in *Roll, Jordan, Roll*, Leslie Howard Owens, in *This Species of Property*, and Herbert Gutman, in *The Black Family in Slavery and Freedom*, found a much more complex story in which enslaved people played a more active role in shaping their own culture, calling Elkins's inter-pretation into question. Robert Fogel and Stanley Engerman brought computer analysis to bear on the issue of the quality of slave life in their influential and controversial *Time on the Cross*. Over the next decade there was a profusion of scholarship on slavery and the antislavery struggle. The field of African American history, for generations largely confined to segregated black public schools and colleges, burst onto the academic scene, bringing new insights to the study of American history, culture, and society. Finally, with Alex Haley's publication of his family history in *Roots* and the TV series that followed, the general public began to hear the voices of African Americans telling their own stories.[5]

In the decades since the 1970s, our understanding of slavery has changed dramatically, and a more complex and compelling picture of the slave experience has emerged. Thanks to groundbreaking work, we now see slavery as a more dynamic institution encompassing many different slave experiences in different times and places. We know that slavery originally existed in all original thirteen colonies, from New Hampshire to South Carolina. We know that before the American Revolution, New York City was second only to Charleston, South Carolina, in British North America as a major center of urban slavery. And we know that the shift in the chief slave crop from tobacco and rice in the eastern South before the Revolution to cotton in the deep South early in the nineteenth century profoundly changed slave life, the national economy, and politics. Debra Gray White showed us that slavery's impact on women was very different from that on men, and Jacqueline Jones gave us a sense of how varied the effects of work were on black women and their families during and after slavery. Peter Kolchin led us to compare the lives of American slaves and Russian serfs, while Phillip D. Morgan showed how the cultures and work of slaves in the Chesapeake region in the eighteenth century differed from those in South Carolina's Lowcountry. Brenda E. Stevenson pointed out the difficulties of maintaining families and the importance of extended kinship in the slave community, and Wilma King focused our attention on the lives of slave children. Ira Berlin's extensive research demonstrated how the Creoles of the Atlantic world became the Charter generation of American slaves, how Africans became African Americans, and how early slave communities were dislocated and disrupted in a second Middle Passage in the nineteenth century.[6]

In *Slavery and the Making of America*, we tell this complex story through the lives and words of the slaves themselves, looking at slavery from the vantage point of the enslaved. We follow individuals from African freedom to American slavery and beyond to freedom again. In the process, we seek to illustrate the inextricable link between American freedom and American slavery. This is a story of intense violence and determined resistance. People were not easily enslaved. Slavery was a coercive system sustained by the mobilization of the entire society, and its maintenance rested on the use of unimaginable violence and the constant threat of violence. It is also an inspiring story about those who would not allow their spirits to be broken by the violence of slavery, those who found ways to create families and communities, and those few who managed to escape to freedom. The story told here goes beyond the life of slavery as a legal institution, to the time after the Civil War when the nation struggled to determine the meaning of freedom for black Americans. It shows the ways that new systems of racial control came to replace the old rules of the slave system and how the system of legal segregation, called Jim Crow, came into existence in the South.

The history of slavery is central to the history of the United States, and so this is also a story about the values and events that shaped American society. White Americans committed to freedom and God-given rights found it necessary to justify their economic system based on slavery. Some could not, and they became part of an enduring campaign to abolish slavery from the country and the world. Others rationalized the contradiction with theories of racial inferiority, arguing that black people were particularly well-suited for enslavement, that they benefited from enslavement or that slavery was necessary for their control. Although slavery was abolished nearly a century and a half ago, the racism rooted in the nation's attempts to justify it remains with us today as the legacy of American slavery.

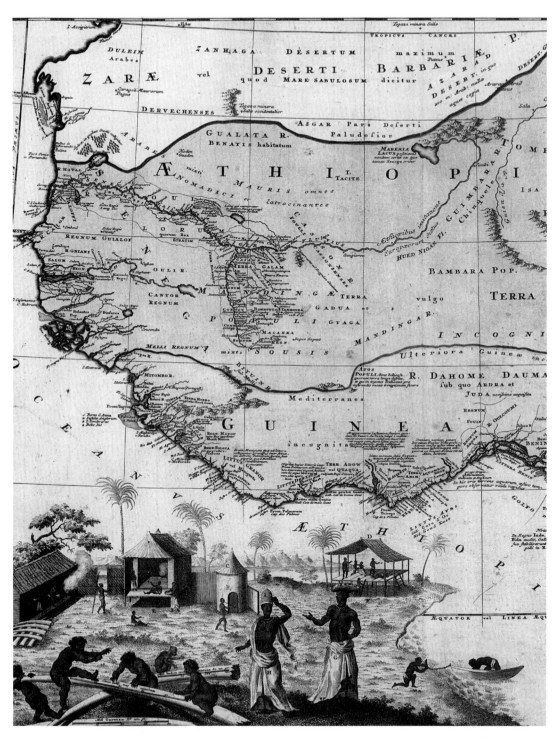

This mid-eighteenth-century map of the west coast of Africa shows the main ports of the slave trade, from present-day Senegal and Gambia in the northwest to Gabon in the southeast. The main commodity was of course Africans themselves, whose domestic and working lives are depicted in the illustration.

The African Roots of Colonial America

1

Just before dawn on a spring morning in 1806, thirteen-year-old Anta Majigeen Njaay was asleep when men on horseback, their long, braided hair flying out behind them, charged into her prosperous West African village in Senegambia, just south of the Sahara Desert. Anta awoke to the terrifying sounds of battle, and by the end of the morning, these frightening men had killed her father, several of her uncles, and many of the village's other men. The invaders were warrior slaves, the special armed force of Amari Ngoone Ndella Kumba, king of Kajor, a coastal kingdom that had risen to power in Senegambia during the eighteenth century, carved out of the old Wolof empire of Jolof. Their job protecting Kajor and its ruler extended to raiding enemy villages and delivering valuable goods to the king. They also took prisoners to be traded to European slave dealers in return for fine fabrics, wines, and weapons. Occasionally, when too few enemies were available for slaves, they raided villages like Anta's, villages supposedly under the king's protection. By noon on the day of the raid, the soldiers had packed up looted goods and rounded up captives, including Anta, her mother, many of her other relatives, and the family servants. Slave traders cared little whether the captives were slaves, free artisans, or nobility like Anta, who was descended from the founder of the Jolof Empire and whose large Njaay family had provided generations of rulers.

Trade between Europe and Africa was centuries old. Ancient trade routes crossed the Sahara from West Africa to the Mediterranean, and Africa supplied most of Europe's gold from as early as the eighth century. Political and technological developments in the fifteenth century combined to change the nature of the trade and increased the importance of West African coastal nations. When the Turks captured Constantinople in 1453, they cut off Europeans' supply of slaves from the Slavic areas around the Black Sea. These slaves had provided the major workforce for the sugar plantations on the Mediterranean islands, so European

An ivory spoon made by the Edo people of the Benin Kingdom in the sixteenth or seventeenth century. The bird with outstretched wings on the spoon's handle is a feature of traditional Benin art. Edo artists also made such artifacts for export to Europe.

sugar producers increasingly looked to Africa for slave labor. Advances in navigation in the fifteenth century enabled the Portuguese to sail to the coast of West Africa, bypassing the Africans controlling the Sahara trade. There, in 1472, the Portuguese negotiated their first slave-trading agreement directly with a king's court, an agreement that included trade for gold and ivory as well. The African–European trade during the next two hundred years was complex: In addition to the trade in slaves and gold, African manufactured goods were exchanged for European manufactured goods. By the eighteenth century, European consumers coveted African textiles; ivory spoons, horns, and saltcellars; and woven mats from Senegambia, often used as bedcovers. Likewise, European textiles and beads were highly valued by fashion-conscious African consumers.[1]

The great empires of Ghana, lasting from the fourth century to the twelfth, and Mali, from the thirteenth century to the late fifteenth, controlled the African–European trade routes. As European nations claimed trade routes in the Atlantic Ocean, and as coastal areas provided new gateways for trade, competition for control of the trade intensified among both European and African nations, and trading dominance was more difficult to maintain. Songhay, the last of the great trading empires in West Africa, which arose in the late fifteenth century, collapsed by the early seventeenth century. The march of sugar cultivation, with its voracious appetite for slave labor, across the Atlantic Ocean to Brazil and the West Indies made the African trade even more lucrative for European nations, and they vied with each other and with African nations in attempts to control the markets. To this end, European nations organized such state-sponsored trading corporations as the Dutch West India Company and Britain's Royal Africa Company and established a string of fortresses along the African coast. One of the first of these fortresses was Elmina, a castle established by the Portuguese in 1481 and held by them until it was taken over by the Dutch in 1637. As the slave trade developed, European nations established more than fifty forts along the three-hundred-mile coastline from the Senegal River to Angola.[2]

Although contending European nations did establish control of the sea trade, they never managed to control the sources of goods and slaves. African nations continued to control the interior of the continent, and a class of private entrepreneurs cooperated with them to dominate the trade along the coast by the late seventeenth century. Many of these middlemen were mixed-race people originally from Cape Verde, an island located off the African coast where the Portuguese had established sugar plantations in the fifteenth century. As European trading activity expanded to the coastal areas of the continent, these people—Africans with intercultural skills and often with an interracial heritage, whom historian Ira Berlin has called Atlantic Creoles—played significant roles in the intercontinental trade. Many worked as agents for the Portuguese or for West African nations and European trading companies. Sometimes they went into business for themselves. By the middle of the eighteenth century the Dutch employed hundreds of mixed-race people as soldiers and trading officials in the trading forts along the Guinea coast. Multilingual and cosmopolitan, with ties to both African and European cultures, these people were invaluable to the commercial enterprises that negotiated vast cultural differences. Generally outcasts in the European societies and denied the right to inherit property, hold land, or marry in African societies, these brown-skinned people developed their own

In the fifteenth and sixteenth centuries Timbuktu was an intellectual and commercial center of the empire of Songhay. A visitor in the sixteenth century said it was "a wonder to see what plentie of Merchandize is daily brought hither and how costly and sumptious all things be.... Here are many shops of... merchants and especially of such as weave linnen."

This seventeenth-century bronze head represented a departed king of the powerful Benin Empire, a society in present-day southern Nigeria rich in artistic expression. It was the centerpiece of an altar for the king's ancestors, which commemorated the power and spiritual presence of past rulers.

subculture, including a synthetic language that became invaluable to trade throughout the Atlantic region. As the African–European trade grew, so did the enclaves of these Atlantic Creoles, expanding beyond the African coast to seaports in Europe and coastal areas of the Americas in the sixteenth and seventeenth centuries.[3]

Some of the best-known Atlantic Creoles were the canoemen who plied their trade carrying goods and people between European ships and coastal trading forts or who organized companies of African canoemen to do the work. By all reports, these men were usually independent merchants for hire to the highest bidder. Canoemen claimed the right to regulate their own work, refusing to venture out when they deemed the surf too rough for safety, when abused by their employer, or when they disputed the conditions of their labor. Because the African coast lacked harbors that could accommodate European ships, the canoemen were indispensable to the African trade.[4]

By the late eighteenth century, trade in weapons and human beings had created more changes in the power structure of West Africa. With guns and gunpowder, the kingdom of Kajor, for example, where Anta lived, developed a military force feared in the region, thereby extending its rule. Indeed, guns were the first European goods introduced into the African trade that Africans did not already produce, although iron had been used in Africa as early as 600 BCE. Long before Europeans arrived in the area south of the Sahara, African iron working produced steel that rivaled in quality the steel produced in Europe many centuries later.[5] The knives, swords, and other weapons made by Senegambian methods were of fine quality, but they could not compete with European guns. Guns were much more deadly, but at first some Africans were reluctant to use them, considering them weapons for cowards, since they didn't require the close-in fighting of earlier weapons. Coastal nations' direct access to European-supplied guns gave them an advantage over inland groups, increased their power, and encouraged efforts to maintain their control of the coastal trade by war if necessary. The nations of Europe and West Africa all maneuvered for maximum trade advantage, playing one competitor off against the others in commercial combat. During the early 1760s, for example, France and Britain competed over the trade with Senegambian rulers and allied themselves with rival warring Senegambian forces. From the African point of view, this was a war to deny Europeans access to inland areas and to determine which Africans would maintain control.

Although Europeans held a great advantage along the coast and along the banks of major rivers, where the heavy guns of their ships protected their positions, they were vulnerable inland beyond the reach of their artillery. European slavers could not remain inland for long, as exposure to such tropical diseases as malaria and yellow fever placed them at great risk. A study of European mortality in seventeenth-century West Africa found that 60 percent died within their first eight months on the continent.[6] The climate of sub-Saharan Africa and the power of African coastal nations combined to keep Europeans largely confined to the coastal trade. Thus, Anta Majigeen Njaay and the other captives from her village, like countless millions of Africans over the four centuries of the Atlantic slave trade, found themselves marched to the coast to be held for European traders. When they arrived at the town of Rufisque at the foot of the Cape Verde peninsula, French- and English-speaking merchants looked them

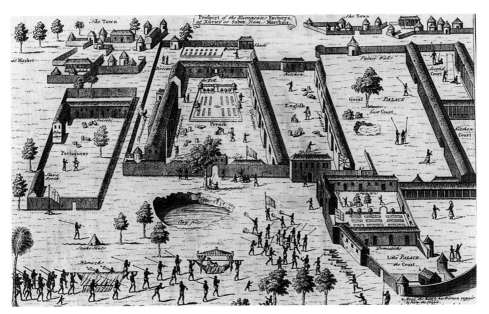

Slave factories on the West African coast were maintained by local kings for various European nations. There African captives from the interior were collected and sold into the Atlantic slave trade.

over and bid for each individually. Anta's group was unusual, with many more women than the normal preponderance of men wanted for heavy labor, but they were sold. Canoemen, with their long narrow canoes, then carried them to the trading fort on the small island of Goree. There, imprisoned in dark cells that opened to courtyards enclosed by high stone walls, they awaited the departure of a vessel bound for the Americas.[7]

Anta's reaction to her plight can only be imagined, since it was not recorded. She was a young girl on the threshold of womanhood, from a prestigious family who was captured and imprisoned along with surviving members of her family and village, including family servants and some of her uncles' slaves. She was familiar with African slavery, but she could not have been prepared for the next stage of her journey. A few other African captives did leave accounts of their experiences. Venture Smith was from Guinea, in the area bordering Africa's Gulf of Guinea. At the age of six, as he recalled, an "army supplied and incited by whites" captured him and marched him to the coast. They imprisoned him there in what he called a castle to await sale. Eventually, traders placed him and 250 others on board a Rhode Island–based ship bound for the British West Indian colony of Barbados. During his capture, the six-year-old had seen his father killed, a trauma that remained with him. As an adult he reported, "The shocking scene is to this day fresh in my memory."[8]

Uncertainty was one of the most distressing parts of another captive's initial enslavement. A small raiding party in Benin, in the eastern region of present-day Nigeria, captured Olaudah Equiano, the eleven-year-old son of an official of the Ibo nation. Although captured and at first enslaved in Africa with his sister, Olaudah later became part of the Atlantic trade, staying a few weeks in Barbados before being transported to Virginia. Once he left Africa, he spent most of his time alone or with Africans who spoke languages different from his own. His experience differed from people who were captured in large groups, and his inability to communicate with fellow captives intensified the shock of his situation.

Anta, Venture, and Olaudah were all children from West Africa, a vast area but only a small portion of an immense continent. Africa contains 11,700,000 square miles, is second only to Asia in size, and is almost six times the size of Europe. From the dry Sahara Desert in the north, an area the size of the United States, to the Kalahari Desert in the south, to the grasslands of the Sudan and tropical rain forests in the central regions, Africa has an extremely varied topography and climate. It is equally diverse in wildlife and human cultures. Africa's ancient civilizations changed partially in response to changes in geography and climate. Between 6000 BCE and 2500 BCE, the northern desert gradually encroached on the existing green belt, driving many societies southward and forcing those who remained to shift from farming to nomadic trading. Equiano's nation and its people were rooted in one of these scattered ancient civilizations. By the end of the fifteenth century, pepper grown in Benin and textiles manufactured there were in great demand in the European market, but by Olaudah's time, Benin's power had been eclipsed by other trading nations in the region. Venture's society in lower Guinea was also partly a product of this southward migration. By the seventeenth century, that region had become a thriving population center, more densely populated than most of Europe at the time.

The diversity of western Africa partly explains Olaudah Equiano's reaction to the things he saw as he reached the coast from his home a hundred miles inland. He was surprised by the ethnic and linguistic diversity of the Africans he met there and amazed by the ocean and the great ships anchored off the coast. His people had been traders, doing business with a number of other national and ethnic groups in the region, but he had never seen such a variety of Africans

European traders purchasing slaves who have been brought to the market yoked together. Often slaves were captured in warfare between competing West African nations and sold for guns and other goods.

as he encountered in the coastal slave-trading markets. He also saw Europeans there for the first time, adding to his confusion. "Their complexions . . . differing so much from ours, their long hair, and the language they spoke (which was very different from any I had ever heard)" all confirmed his fear that he would be killed by these "white men with horrible looks, red faces and long hair" whom he considered "bad spirits."[9]

Olaudah Equiano's fear and confusion were typical of the reaction of Africans brought from inland areas. His greatest relief came from finding an African with whom he could communicate, someone who helped him understand his situation. The white men would take him far away to their country in one of the huge ships, he was told. This was much better than he had feared. Having heard stories of cannibals, he was initially convinced that these strange men were going to eat him, apparently a common fear among those who had never before seen Europeans. According to contemporary observers, "slaves near the coast . . . know what to expect, but those from the interior are terrified by not knowing the purpose [of the trade]." As one eighteenth-century English trader noted, many captives from the more remote areas of the Senegambia region "imagined that all who were sold for slaves were generally eaten or murdered, since none ever returned."

Even well into the nineteenth century, white cannibalism remained a part of West African folklore. Apparently some assumed that the European style of kissing was a part of this cannibalistic tendency.[10] According to Equiano, the captives' fear of white cannibalism persisted during the entire voyage and remained so great even after their arrival in the West Indies that "at last the white people got some old slaves from the land to pacify us. They told us we were not to be eaten but to work, and were soon to go on land where we should see many of our country people. This report eased us much."[11] As a slave of white men, Equiano hoped, life might be no worse for him than for slaves in his homeland. Still, he was worried because "the white people looked and acted . . . in so savage a manner, for I had never seen among any people such instances of brutal cruelty."[12]

Most Africans understood slavery, since slavery was an ancient institution that had been established in North and West Africa before European involvement in the trade. In West Africa, land was not held as private property, and slavery, the ownership of other human beings and their labor, was a major basis of wealth. Slaves thus had measurable value, and trading in slaves was a part of commerce.

Those held in bondage were commonly captured in war, both fighters and their family members. Africans generally sold such captives to Europeans. Pacheco Pereira, a sixteenth-century Portuguese slave trader, commented on taking slaves in Benin, Equiano's homeland. Apparently, at the time, Benin was "usually at war with its neighbors [sic] and taking many captives, whom we buy at 12 or 15 brass bracelets each or for copper bracelets which they prize more." Slaves' value generally increased as

Herman Moll's 1714 map of "Africa Ancient and Modern." The abundant detail is indicative of Europe's keen interest in the opportunities offered by trade and military adventure in Africa.

they were farther from home, the distance making rescue or escape more difficult and political ties in the society less likely. Once on the coast, Pereira reported, the slaves were traded for gold.[13]

Before the fifth century, Romans were willing to pay high prices for North African slaves, largely because of the remoteness of their homelands. Muslims in the Middle East or North Africa especially valued slaves from far away as "strangers" who might be provided with trusted positions because they were thought to have no local loyalties other than to their masters. Masters often used these slaves as special military guards for households or harems. Slaves might be seen as less suitable for slavery as they became more familiar with the social customs and the politics of a region. Thus, the slaveholders might see children raised in the local society as unfit for slavery and release them from bondage. In such ancient kingdoms as Egypt in the north and Ghana and its successor Mali just to the south, slavery was an integral part of society. Slaves provided labor for a wide variety of tasks, including farming, clearing land, skilled wood or metal work, and domestic service. Holding slaves was also a sign of individual and national wealth and power. In some areas—such as along

continues on page 24

The Middle Passage: An Eyewitness Account

Olaudah Equiano was kidnapped from his home in Essaka, an Ibo village in present-day Nigeria, at age eleven, transported to the Atlantic coast, and sold into slavery. He was the first American slave to write an autobiography telling of his experiences. Published in 1791, the book became a sensation and was printed in nine different editions before Equiano died in 1797. He and his book were valuable resources for the early abolition movement. The following is his account of the horrors of the Middle Passage.

At last, when the ship we were in had got in all her cargo, they made ready with many fearful noises, and we were all put under deck, so that we could not see how they managed the vessel. But this disappointment was the least of my sorrow. The stench of the hold while we were on the coast was so intolerably loathsome, that it was dangerous to remain there for any time, and some of us had been permitted to stay on the deck for the fresh air; but now that the whole ship's cargo were confined together, it became absolutely pestilential. The closeness of the place, and the heat of the climate, added to the number in the ship, which was so crowded that each had scarcely room to turn himself, almost suffocated us. This produced copious perspirations, so that the air soon became unfit for respiration, from a variety of loathsome smells, and brought on a sickness among the slaves, of which many died, thus falling victims to the improvident avarice, as I may call it, of their purchasers. This wretched situation was again aggravated by the galling of the chains, now become insupportable; and the filth of the necessary tubs, into which the children often fell, and were almost suffocated. The shrieks of the women, and the groans of the dying, rendered the whole a scene of horror almost inconceivable. Happily perhaps for myself I was soon reduced so low here that it was thought necessary to keep me almost always on deck; and from my extreme youth I was not put in fetters. In this situation I expected every hour to share the fate of my companions, some of whom were almost daily brought upon deck at the point of death, which I began to hope would soon put an end to my miseries. Often did I think many of the inhabitants of the deep much more happy than myself; I envied them the freedom they enjoyed, and as often wished I could change my condition for theirs. Every circumstance I met with served only to render my state more painful, and heighten my apprehensions, and my opinion of the cruelty of the whites. . . .

One day, when we had a smooth sea, and a moderate wind, two of my wearied countrymen, who were chained together (I was near them at the time), preferring death to such a life of misery, somehow made through the nettings, and jumped into the sea: immediately another quite dejected fellow, who, on account of his illness, was suffered to be out of irons, also followed their example; and I believe many more would soon have done the same, if they had not been prevented by the ship's crew, who were instantly alarmed. Those of us that were the most active were, in a moment, put down under the deck; and there was such a noise and confusion amongst the people of the ship as I never heard before, to stop her, and get the boat to go out after the slaves. However, two of the wretches were drowned, but they got the other, and afterwards flogged him unmercifully, for thus attempting to prefer death to slavery. In this manner we continued to undergo more hardships than I can now relate; hardships which are inseparable from this accursed trade.[1]

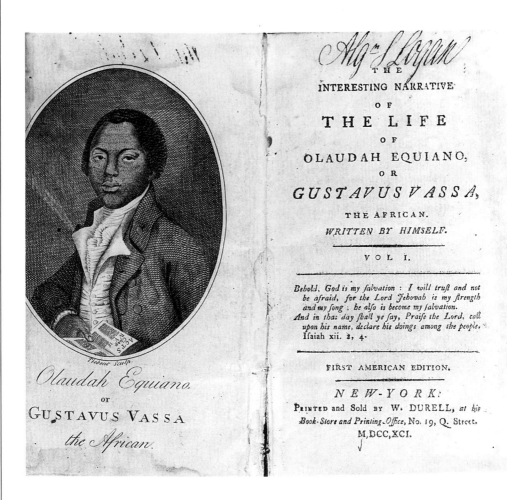

continued from page 21

the Gold Coast, the region of West Africa along the Atlantic coast between the Komoe and Volta Rivers—only people of high social status could hold slaves.[14] Slaves, as property, could be a source of national, as well as personal, display. Between 1312 and 1332 Mali's great Muslim leader, Mansa Kango Musa, made regular pilgrimages to the holy city of Mecca. His camel caravans were weighed down with a thousand pounds of gold, were escorted by armies of servants and slaves wielding heavy golden staffs, and were calculated to impress rival states.[15] In terms of wealth, governmental organization, and military power, fourteenth-century Mali dominated its region and rivaled any nation in Europe.

African slavery could be brutal, but seldom did African masters hold life and death power over their slaves. Often slaves were people with acknowledged rights, and slavery frequently was paternalistic, in that masters had recognized responsibilities toward their slaves. In the Kongo empire of Central Africa the word "*nleke*" was used for both slave and child. Theoretically, slaves were treated as permanently subordinate family members with special responsibilities, the equivalent of perpetual children. In some societies slaves could own property, had the choice of marriage partners, and could even own their own slaves. One European observer of slavery in Anta Njaay's homeland, Senegambia, reported that agricultural slaves were allowed to work one day a week for themselves and their families. State officials often believed the undivided loyalty of slaves suited them for military and administrative service. Slaves could face harsh conditions and cruel punishment for disciplinary infractions, but African slavery contrasted greatly with the institution that developed in the Americas. Indeed, historian John Thornton has concluded that the life of an African slave was often comparable to the life of a European free tenant or hired worker.[16]

The slavery in the Americas that Anta Njaay, Venture Smith, and Olaudah Equiano faced was a different and ultimately a more devastating institution than that known in Africa. Equiano's reaction to being held by Europeans reflected his concerns about their plans. As he recalled, "Indeed such were the horrors of my view and fears at the moment, that if ten thousand worlds had been my own, I would have freely parted with them all to have exchanged my condition with that of the meanest slave in my own country."[17] Once taken to the coast, however, African captives were not likely ever to see their homes again. Their period of confinement in coastal forts varied, lasting until ships arrived to take them on to the Americas. Equiano explained the horrible conditions during this six- to eight-week journey known as the "Middle Passage." He reported that some of the children were allowed to remain on the ship's deck until the voyage got under way, but then all slaves were forced below decks, chained together in a tight space under conditions no human being should ever have to endure. "The heat of the climate, added to the number in the ship, which was so crowded that each had scarcely room to turn himself, almost suffocated us," he recalled.[18]

Under these harsh conditions some decided that death might be preferable. One enslaved African recalled being sick with dysentery and unable to eat for days. Many others decided not to eat at all, whereupon their captors often resorted to such tortures as thumbscrews, burning their lips with hot coals, or using force-feeding devices in attempts to prevent their suicide by starvation. Though some slaves did starve themselves to death, others found opportunities during brief respites on deck to jump overboard and drown, perhaps preferring to return home in spirit rather than endure enslavement.[19]

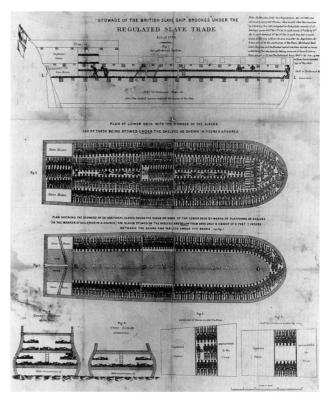

The deck plan of the British slave ship Brookes *illustrates the inhuman method of transporting slaves, effectively making them human cargo. This broadside, published by the British Abolitionist Society in 1789, was a highly effective propaganda tool for the antislavery movement.*

One British surgeon who traveled on a slave ship from West Africa to the West Indies a generation after Equiano's experience confirmed the deplorable conditions. Slaves were locked in irons that were attached to a long chain fixed to the lower deck, binding fifty or sixty men to the ship and to one another. At one point when the doctor ventured below decks to attend the sick, he was forced to step on chained bodies, as slaves covered the entire floor. He reported that slaves were fed "chiefly of horse beans, boiled to the consistency of a pulp;

of boiled yams and rice, and sometimes of a small quantity of beef and pork."[20] Depending on the weather, twice a day, at about eight in the morning and four in the afternoon, slaves were allowed above decks for food and exercise. This minimal privilege was permitted not as an entitlement but as a means of protecting the value of the slave cargo. Even so, records of this Atlantic slave trade reveal that mortality rates were generally about 15 percent and could range as high as one-third of the slaves during this Middle Passage.

Life aboard a slave ship was unbearable and often deadly for the slaves, but it was also dangerous for slave ship crews. They faced the hazardous job of all sailors and the threat of tropical diseases. Angry slaves posed additional dangers. "The Negroes [fight] like wild beasts," warned one veteran slave trader. "Slavery is a dangerous Business at sea as well as ashore."[21] Mortality among slave ship crews, some of whom were unpaid workers impressed into service or convicts serving on the crew in lieu of a prison term, was almost as high as among the slaves, although it did decline over the course of the eighteenth century. A number of captains lost their lives in slave revolts on their ships, a danger even if the revolt was unsuccessful. Heavily armed sailors generally managed to quell shipboard rebellions, but a notable few were successful. Several days out from the Guinea Coast of Africa en route to Rhode Island in 1730, slaves aboard the *Little George* managed to kill three crewmen and subdue and imprison the captain and the rest of the crew. The slaves sailed the ship back to Sierra Leone and negotiated with the captain, exchanging the freedom of the ninety-six slaves for the freedom of the captain and crew.[22] Investors were willing to chance the risks of this inhuman enterprise because profits

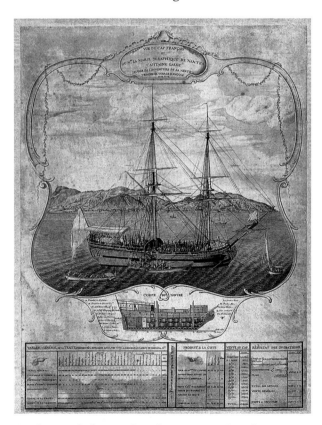

On the French slave-trading ship La Marie-Séraphique, *an iron fence was constructed to confine the enslaved Africans when they were on deck.*